1.95

Herbert F. Brokering

Drawings by Art Kirchhoff

Concordia

Publishing House
St. Louis

Concordia Publishing House, St. Louis, Missouri
Copyright © 1977 Concordia Publishing House

MANUFACTURED IN THE UNITED STATES OF AMERICA

Library of Congress Cataloging in Publication Data

Brokering, Herbert F
    Lord, if.

    1. Meditations. I. Title.
BV4832.2.B743   242'.4   76-51852
ISBN 0-570-03046-3

To Honor my Mother and Father, Clara and Heinrich Brokering, who first brought me the Gospel imperative.

Lord,
if
Your friends could come back
so often,
and if kings and queens had so many chances,
then
it's clear to me
that I can have many moods,
I can be cocoon and butterfly,
I can have a winter and
then a spring,
I can have hot and cold feelings,
I can fly and crash,
and I can come back.

Lord,
if
You made the spirit,
the breath, the wind, the soul,
then
let me marvel more at imagination,
flight of fantasy, the unusual, the accidental,
and the feelings and faith
that come seemingly from out of nowhere,
and go on,
through me.

Lord,
if
shepherds could be amazed,
and kings could travel so far to find You,
and friends broke bread to remember You
and expect Your return,
then
I need the faith of the child,
the right to wish,
the ability to dream and build sand castles,
the nerve to break them down
and build them over,
the hope to know what is not reasonable,
and to lean into your promise.

Lord,
if
I am to ever rest in some tomb or place,
then
help me see beyond it,
even as now I can see my past
and marvel.

Lord,
if
I am to stay in community,
then keep me in touch with newborn babies,
the miracle of their most early life,
their deep silent habits,
their strong instincts,
their trust,
for I too came from there.

Lord,
if
we are saved in Baptism
through a death in the water,
and if the worst is past,
the death is done,
and the deep sea has given us up
as it did release Jonah,
then
let us behave as though saved,
and tell You thanks.

Lord,
if
I am the only one,
unique,
different from any before or ever to come,
then
take away my competitive spirit,
and any war against others,
for they too are unique.

Lord,
if
I am not to be lost,
then
keep me conscious of my deep roots,
childhood joy still alive,
soul and spirit still longing,
and hope as old as forefathers
and prophets.

Lord,
if
I can feel both woe and joy in me,
both the ouch and hurray in me,
then
I know the elastic inside myself
which keeps me from breaking in two.

Lord,
if
I live never to touch a star,
or fathom the hot vapors of Your burning sun,
yet have them as my own brother and sister,
then
I will be sure again,
each day,
that I am part of Your whole creation.

Lord,
if
I am to get in or out of the many parades
going on, showing off,
marching and ending,
then
show me what I'm in and why.

Lord,
if
I think of all the parts of the one body,
or any person or living thing,
then I am dumbfounded,
I marvel at how it all holds together,
and how what could be chaos and tension
turns so quickly to peace.

Lord,
if
I am to shout Your name,
and name You the Lord of all,
then
teach me to shout loud and soft,
depending on the situation,
and to know how sensitive it is
to hear Your name.

Lord,
if
You could cause the broken-hearted to sing psalms,
to ask for remembrance,
and see the lost come back running,
then
sin and sorrow, and iron vaults
will not conquer me.

Lord,
if
mountains can hold deep scars inside their centers
and bear creative marks for eons,
then I too can contain the deep marks
of Your creative force
and Spirit.

Lord,
if
You can help a stranger
sort through her feelings of wanting and craving,
and put her guilty mind at peace,
then
I can be down
or torn
and know You come there to ask me
what I need to answer.

Lord,
if
You can trust Your grace
in the life of a baby in Bethlehem,
in a time of leprosy, disease,
and civil strife,
then
I will thank You doubly
for the times in which I am,
for medication,
and safety when I am sick.

Lord,
if
You can know when a sparrow falls,
and the number of hairs on the head,
then
You know where I'm coming from,
going,
and that I can make it.

Lord,
if
You did break the rules to heal,
and tear down dead tradition to live the Gospel,
then
nothing will imprison Your Gospel
in my world
or in Your people.

Lord,
if
You did keep Your grace going
in the lives of outcasts,
and did break bread at their tables,
then
there is no time or place
in which You will not eat or be
with me.

Lord,
if
by Moses You put Your hand on waters
to part them,
and if You
lower Your voice into the deep of oceans,
raise and call those drowned,
then
You can get through to me
with Your hand and voice
and power.

Lord,
if
breeze can come and go
with constant seasons in between,
and meadows can break into a solid blue,
and storms can go completely out of sight,
then
I will say yes more easily,
and marvel at the unraveling of Creation,
and the unveiling of Your grace.

Lord,
if
You can open tombs on Easter,
and in the same kind of quake
swallow cities,
bury villages under hot ashes,
then
I will love Your mercy
and trust
the justice of Your judgment.

Lord,
if
You can make life so intricate,
and meaning so interwoven,
and us so interdependent,
then
close the gaps between us
and nature,
so we reenter each day as a new creation
and as a whole.

Lord,
if
You did take on so much to do,
and if so much can go on and on
without any worry,
and be so consistent and continuous,
then
we can take care of each other
more than we know, and
we have more going for us
than we can imagine.

Lord,
if
You can come in glory
and keep us so intrigued
and guessing and happy and confident,
then
give me more feeling for the uncertain
and for the sure.

Lord,
if
You can own the whole universe at once,
and make glaciers so hard and then soft,
and keep the energy flow going,
then
You can warm a cold conversation
and break the ice between people.

Lord,
if
You can keep your trust with everything,
and Your contract with the dead,
then
I can hear You in the midst of absolute despair,
and will not give up,
when things are as bad as possible
and I am all the way down.

Lord,
if
You will keep breath alive from age to age,
and keep the commonplace and miracles going
in the same hour,
then
I can view life as natural and miraculous,
and simple and spectacular,
and myself as saint and sinner.

Lord,
if
You can surprise a prophet in a storm,
a harlot at a well,
a robber on a cross,
a mother at a banquet,
then
You will come to me in a room, on a spot,
under a cloud,
or beside a table.

Lord,
if
You can come through codes and secret messages,
through signs,
masks,
prison language, and exile,
then
You can hear my private codes,
uncover inner feelings,
and search my secret desires.

Lord,
if
You can take it easy on Your seventh day
and trust it all,
and let it go on
and let it all unwind,
then
I will not hold on so tight,
and not be so on edge,
and will let the inside of me escape,
and find the power of rest
in trust.

Lord,
if
You can turn Your earth into pastures,
into wool and silk,
Your earth to roses and daffodils,
Your earth to gold and bright bronze,
Your earth to yellow tips of grain,
then
renew in us a high regard for earth
and farms, for sections of soil,
for fallow land,
for swamps and lowland,
and for topsoil.

Lord,
if
electronic music can make so many combinations,
and if there are so many themes and moods
in harmony and rhythm,
then
surely You are more generous than I act, more flexible
than we can ever imagine,
and as understanding as I need.

Lord,
if
You can put together light and night,
atmosphere and land,
and bring peace from all the parts,
then
You can put together for us
what seems so separate,
span that which is so distant,
and make us marvel at what is so close.

Lord,
if
You can pull a man over a wall to save him,
a nation out of a raging sea,
a world out of a Flood,
then
You can pull me
through,
up,
and over.

Lord,
if
You can make creation in an order
so that nature unfolds
as by itself
and one thing leads into another,
then
keep me
in the unfolding nature of events,
the flow of life forms,
and in the continuous energy
of Your creation.

Lord,
if
You can bring nations back to the same rocks,
the same mountains,
the same trees,
to the same tunes,
and there rekindle their spirits
in this return,
then
make us more aware of the value of returning,
of the joy in recollection,
and the magnificence of memory.

Lord,
if
You can form
and stir enough energy and substance
in the beginning
to last all this time,
then
give us the desire to toy with Your mystery,
discover Your miracles,
and reconsider as gift all energy.

Lord,
if
in the pouring of the cup
and
in the drinking
we have a taste of the feast to come,
then
help me enjoy the drink even more,
expect the meal yet to come,
and imagine being at the table with You.

Lord,
if
You can walk through a locked door,
surprise a fearful huddle of disciples,
and simply say,
"It is I,"
then
there is no door of mine
that keeps You out,
no doubt that can keep Your voice quiet,
and no fear that can keep me
from hearing You.

Lord,
if
You are so known and honored for giving,
healing, and restoring hope,
then
I can increase my will to give,
my trust in others,
my feeling for enemies,
and my imagination for a torn world.

Lord,
if
Your creation is
still setting life
into motion,
if creating is a long-lasting verb,
and if
You made it all
to be a continuous process,
then
let me see myself as part
of Your original creation,
unfolding inside the miracle of
Your loving power.

Lord,
if
You are ahead of us,
and also coming to meet us,
then
we are somewhere between,
and we have You both coming to us
and going.

Lord,
if
You break up mountains from below,
break open a winter early,
crack a seed on time,
then
You can lift me
from any
grave.

Lord,
if
You are always
with us,
and
never leave
or forsake
us,
then
Your Lord's day
cuts through
all the days of the week,
and worship
is indeed
a continual
act.

Lord,
if
You could cause
grace
through droughts and floods
and cause
universes to begin new cycles,
then
You can supervise what I do,
bless it,
make it work
or not,
and You can close down a job
or build it up.

Lord,
if
You can kneel to pray for all of us
in a night,
and beg so much
for strangers
and us yet unborn,
and beseech so
in behalf of Your enemies,
then
remove from me
the feeling of being forgotten,
abandoned,
and rejected.

Lord,
if
You could let a city ruler keep after You,
pleading,
when his daughter was dying,
and if he could beg
when You were so busy,
and keep begging and believing
when the girl was dead,
then
I will beg You and
believe You
and not give up.

Lord,
if
You can take a dead girl
by the hand
and tell her to arise
as if from her sleep,
then
I can see
how quick and amazing
my resurrection will be.

Lord,
if
we can wear crosses and robes
and decorate them
so delicately,
and can buy crosses
for their detail and shades
and hidden vines and branches,
then
help us cherish our own history
in some of its exciting details.

Lord,
if
You taught in open fields,
at mealtimes,
while harvesting,
while on the walk,
while watching birds fly
and nest,
while farmers planted and weeded,
then
put my mind and faith at ease
in all kinds of ordinary,
extraordinary,
holy places.

Lord,
if
You can make pearls
inside oysters,
in the deep
dark
bottom of oceans,
then
you can make me
precious
when I am deep,
down,
and under.

Lord,
if
by fire You led people
at night,
revealed what they could never guess,
make clear
what was strange,
make new what seemed dead,
then
let this fire of Yours
come over
and into me
with warmth
and with light.

Lord,
if
birds can be used
to describe the Kingdom,
and can carry messages
to Noah
and food to hungry prophets,
and if birds can be a sign
at Your own baptism,
then
help us read
some of Your great messages
through birds,
and think of trust,
freedom, and presence.

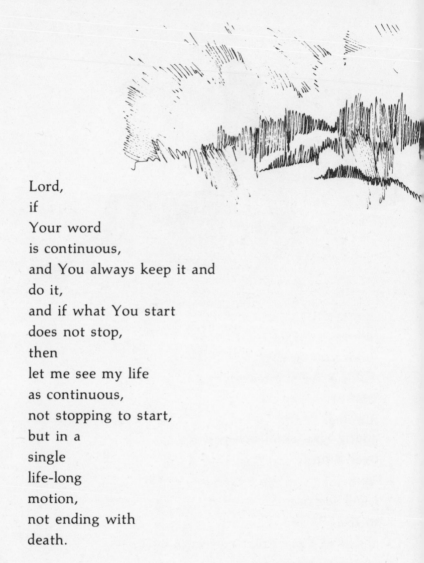

Lord,
if
Your word
is continuous,
and You always keep it and
do it,
and if what You start
does not stop,
then
let me see my life
as continuous,
not stopping to start,
but in a
single
life-long
motion,
not ending with
death.

Lord,
if
Your resurrection
began
a new calendar
and if You have such power
over time,
then
I will see time as Your gift
to me,
and that You came to save
me from being either
enemy or slave
of time.

Lord,
if
I could once
cartwheel over graves,
over sick beds,
over starving children,
and over my own guilt,
then
maybe I could learn
how to laugh
and trust
in this sometimes terrifying world.

Lord,
if
I could play a horn or fiddle,
and travel the earth with no word
but only the sound of songs,
then
I believe I could carry Your Gospel
through wood and wind,
and it would be known.

Lord,
if
the grave did not hold You,
and the earth
could not contain You,
then
there is more ahead
for me
than I can even imagine.

Lord,
if
You are King of Creation
and the One
who keeps life continuous,
then
remind me of the wonder of my body,
the secret codes in genes,
the inheritance
that comes to me and goes through me,
the particles and atoms
that make me visible
for these few years,
and stir me enough
to say thanks
on my own.

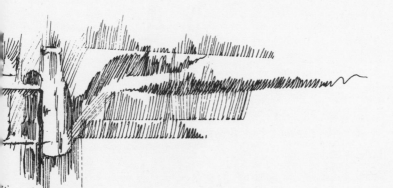

Lord,
if
those of old
could dream and wish,
and write songs about birds in flight
and men stuck in mud,
then
get my mind to focus on Your creation,
strong currents in wind streams,
tugs and pulls of wind on kites,
migrations by secret maps
in temperature and air currents,
and the marvel of imagination,
without losing touch
with self.

Lord,
if
You can pick up nations
and give them a hundred good years,
and kingdoms
and give them golden years,
then
I know again
You can give me rest
when I am exhausted,
peace when I am scared,
forgiveness when I am guilty,
and protection
when I am overcome.

Lord,
if
You are from everlasting,
then
show me the deep meaning
of the deep,
deep space,
deep past,
deep thoughts,
deep future, and
deep forgiveness.

Lord,
if
Your creation is
a mixture of all elements,
then
show me the power of mixing honey
with dough,
dipping bread
into wine,
uniting water with Your word,
the benediction and the sign of the cross,
and all those mixtures
of the sublime and the supreme.

Lord,
if
Your creation is still unfolding,
and You are still releasing the power
of Your might,
then
put me in love
with the fountains that break out of nowhere,
deep hidden rivers,
silent seas under deserts,
and magnify the wonder and wishing
of unfolding inside myself.

Lord,
if
You can wait through dark ages,
and wait centuries for heresies to stop,
and wait many decades for reformations,
and wait for whole nations to repent,
and wait for descendents to return
to their forefather's faith,
then
I know You will wait for me
when I make You wait.

Lord,
if
people could be amazed, baffled,
dumbfounded,
surprised and satisfied so much,
then
I can be surprised
where I am.

Lord,
if
You can wander with Israel for forty years,
and zigzag through their desert
with their complaining,
then
You can stay with me
if my walk gets long,
and the sand is hot under my feet,
and if I complain for any reason at all.

Lord,
if
You can give old Moses one long look
into the Promised Land
before his death,
then
You can take me to high vistas
where I can have the joy of seeing
what only You can promise
and keep.

Lord,
if
You can turn sand and sores into pearls,
hurt into healing,
patience into a party,
and death into resurrection,
then
You will help me to be creative
with what troubles me
the most.

Lord,
if
breaking bread and fish makes it belong to more,
and if the breaking can multiply the love
among us,
and if dividing it is a uniting force,
then
I see a new meaning in Holy Communion,
and in offering.

Lord,
if
there are symbols as old as history,
and if there are meanings universal,
and if people everywhere
imagine some of the same feelings and ideas,
then
a great feeling of oneness and awe
comes over me.

Lord,
if
You trust Your Gospel with kings who murdered,
friends who lied,
nations who whimpered,
and a prophet who cried a lot,
then
I know Your Gospel can also live through me.

Lord,
if
You could break the hold of demons,
break the raging of storms,
break the anger of enemies,
and break the laws against lepers,
then
You can break through thick walls that
separate us here.

Lord,
if
wind is a sign of Your Spirit,
and breath a sign of Your life among us,
then
let us feel more near You
in the evening breezes,
in storms,
and in the breath of our own bodies.

Lord,
if
You could baffle Your closest friends,
confuse Your own mother,
and stump wise men and professors,
then
quiet my own spirit
when I too do not understand
or even move against You.

Lord,
if
You ate fish
as a sign of Your reality after Easter,
and if the disciples needed proof
and Thomas had to see and feel Your scars
to be sure,
then
forgive me for asking twice
and needing proof.

Lord,
if
You can trust Your own Word with storytellers,
translators,
and printings through the ages,
then
You can surely trust in the lives of us
who are worried and unkind,
and I can trust Your own Word
in me.

Lord,
if
it was in the dark that You were born,
supped, prayed, died,
and saved a whole nation going through a sea,
then
surely I must rethink the wonder of Your night,
and mystery of the dark.

Lord,
if
the sign of the cross is upon me
and some water and Your Word creates a miracle,
and if the people present
keep the miracle alive,
then
I am part of a powerful, miraculous people.

Lord,
if
the signature of the cross on my forehead
is a sign of salvation,
then
You are truly simple and profound,
uncomplicated,
and You are quicker than lightning.

Lord,
if
people could run away
and receive promises,
run away and have visions,
run away and be welcome back home,
then
I am not so afraid
of being too lost.

Lord,
if
I am to keep promises,
then
open my senses, focus my spirit,
hear my anger, see my fear,
send me friends,
and keep telling Your promise
to me.

Lord,
if
I know there is a way up,
then I can take the way down,
and I can go under
if You lift me up
as sure as You raise up spring
and open buds on trees.

Lord,
if
in the breaking of bread You can join me
to all those alive,
and to all children yet unborn,
to good weather,
good laws ruling all food,
to the whole church and all saints,
then
I have a new understanding
of the dimension of
Communion.

Lord,
if
thirst is real and wells are dry,
and dust still blows into eyes and mouths and cups,
and some lips are very parched,
then
stir my heart to care more
about the drink I have
and the thirst You quench.

Lord,
if
a child can draw its mother
without looking up,
and draw its father when he is away,
then
help me to imagine more quickly
who You are,
more than how You look.

Lord,
if
long history can create images,
and icons can carry such long feelings and facts
about faith,
and paintings can become classic,
and pictures can reach out to me,
then
help me be more quiet
to hear and to see images.